Of All The Words I Could Write

Valerie Angel

Presentation by *BookLeaf Publishing*

Web: www.bookleafpub.com

E-mail: info@bookleafpub.com

ISBN: 9789394788381

First edition 2022

DEDICATION

This book is dedicated to myself and for myself. For being able to step outside of comfort zones, embark on new journeys in life, and to for being able to pick myself up when all seemed so bleak.

ACKNOWLEDGEMENT

I would like to thank all those who have lived in my heart, and for those who had to move along.

Take Me To The Moon

Please take me to the moon
We wouldn't need much
Just a helmet and some air for two
Because oxygen up there is few

Take me to the moon
Anywhere but here on Earth
Maybe life there would be kind
A few alien friends, I wouldn't mind

Please take me to the moon
Or send me off into the stars
Much rather drive spaceships than cars
Just take me to the moon
And I beg, make it soon!

Friends from the Compost

I wish I were a worm
In dirt, all day long, I would play
Making friends with the beetles
Throwing parties with the spiders
A fresh cup of coffee grinds in the morning
Or perhaps a cup before bed
But come to think of it,
What is time to a worm anyway?
So maybe there'll be no morning or night
To the life so lived by the worm
Encased in a glistening pink neat
Surrounded by all the vegetables one could eat
So a worm I'd be
No other insect for me

Dear Spider

I'm sorry, dear Spider
For you see,
You have spun your web
Right where I need to be

But you mustn't fret
And you mustn't worry
I saw you quite in time
So neither of us be sorry

Lizard in Solitude

Forgive me there, Lizard
I only came here to write
Please accept my apology
For giving you such a fright

Go on your merry business
And I shall do the same
Basking in each other's company
Our reasons neither be in vain

We hide out here in solitude
But are never really alone
Enjoying the peace of the Tree
And the face upon the Stone

And Thank Heavens

Pardon me,
Dear, Silk Worm
I almost did not see
You spinning so

Too fine for human eyes
Held fast, only for thee
Almost to your demise
Had I not stopped in time

But you see,
How lucky are we
That I stopped for thee
And now my conscience is clear
And thank heavens, you are still here

Two Crows Go Flying By

Two crows go flying by
Across a clear blue sky
Swimming through air
In a tandem pair

Two crows go flying near
Black velvet wings high above
With eyes set on silver
But two hearts made of gold

Two crows are traveling through
Which direction?
I only wish I knew
Soulmates indeed, so far and few

Oh, To be Something

Oh, to be a river
And oh, to be a tree
Moving right along
Pleasant as can be

Oh, to be a fish
And oh, to be a bird
Limitless and free
Never a worry to be heard

Oh, to be a worm
And oh, to be a snake
Gliding upon the earth
Part of each crust that breaks

Oh, to be a planet
And oh, to be a star
Looking down on Earth
Out there, impeccably far

Oh, to be the Sun
And oh, to be the Moon
Star-crossed lovers indeed
I think I should swoon...

Oh, to be something
And oh, to be anything
Other than being human
And so much more than any king

The Poems She Wrote

Oh, the poems she wrote
Of far off places
Only her mind could find
Broken hearts
Those tattered souls
Bound to the confines
Of her glorious page
The poems she wrote,
Brave to the touch
Her words knew no limit
They echo on this very page…

Please?

Please leave me alone,
Just let me be
Can't I heal me?

Please leave me alone,
Just let me be
All this, I could see
My dreams are for me

Please leave me alone
Amd let me be
Leave my dreams, for me

Three Cups

Three cups at your table
But there isn't one for me
I no longer exist in the game of three
But was it ever meant to last?

Three cups at your table
And there isn't one for me
It was never just a "we"
A dream, too quaint to last

Three cups at your table
But no longer one for me
We could have been kindred
Alas, you had to flee

My Heart's Sore

Her sister stops to see my reaction
Some sort of physical indication
That I indeed miss you so
She drops your name casually at first
Then interjects the name a second time
More pronounced than the first
I see her round eyes side gaze
But I do not falter my state of being
I continue on my business
As if the name of rare crystal
Means very little to me
Because no one need know
The way I miss you so
Then I remember, I have hurt worse before
So you moving on
Simply adds to my heart's sore

Romance is Finest with a Never

Every time I think of reaching out
It's always early morning, your time
But here, for me
It's nearly dusk,
A perfect time to think of you...

And if I ever get the courage to reach out, then
I should think it be night but who are we to
fight,
About a lost chance of love,
That has since been absolved
Although is it really ever?
Romance is finest with a never

Frayed

I laughed,
Then she laughed,
We laughed on together

I went,
Then she went too,
We went there together

I loved,
And she loved,
We both loved together

But I stayed,
And then she left,
A friendship since frayed

I Know

I know you still think of me
You tell me in my dreams
I know you still speak of me
The smoke exposes your secrets

SCORPIO

I hope the pain of my absence
Eats you alive
I hope your heart breaks
Every time you remember me
I hope your mind becomes ablaze
When my memory crosses your mind
I hope you stand alone in the mirror,
And soak in all the guilt
I hope when you light up your smoke
You go up in the flames

A Simple Fellow

He walks past me
And he stares...
You can see,
Confusion in his eyes
A faint hint of memory too
But he cannot seem to place
My tired and often somber face

I know he knows me
This much is true
But to his plain eye,
I am so unreconsinzble without you
If your face,
Was here next to mine
I think he would remember just fine

If then,
And only then
He may approach with a 'hello'
But he won't
And I could careless
This is a heartbreak
Much to complex for a simple fellow

Sealed Fate in Black Blood

You're stuck with me, forever,
A sealed fate,
Rested upon your left shoulder
The black blood,
Runs beneath your skin
Just as much as mine
Stamped in the shape of a hand
And so now,
Every time you look
Upon that very shoulder
Your heart will have to remember
A friendship you left to smolder

This Libra

This Libra longs for love
As wind longs
For the flight of Doves
Both providing peace
Along with a sense of hope
How else would we cope?
Through tear drops and smoke
Through words on a paper
And nights filled with sleepless slumber
Our bodies, they grow more numb
But our hearts remain true
We can never quite forget
Our true nature is this:
We long for love,
To give love
And to be loved
To be in love,
And so too does the Dove

A Friend Like Toad

I used to have a friend
A friend like Frog had Toad
A kindred soul, indeed
Walking on that never ending road

As Frog and Toad would
So would we
Skipping stones,
And playing amongst the trees

Just as Frog had Toad
I had her
And she had me
Awe, how lucky were we !

Cosmic Bond

I felt a heart string pull today
And I know it came from you
It came from the room
In my heart, that belonged to you

I felt a heart string pull today
And oh, how it seemed to tug
A thought of you flashed before me
A cosmic type of hug

I felt a heart string pull today
Transcending every bond
Though the bonds may have broken
The universal sign of love has spoken

My Blank Mind

A blank mind,
Runs wild
Driving to the end of town
Nowhere, fast...

A blank mind,
Screams through your head
Echoing off the blank page
With empty white staring back at you

A blank mind,
Interrupts sanity
Or perhaps the sanity interrupts the blank
Even to cross out the other

A blank mind,
Is what you are reading now
From nothing this has come
And from nothing this will go...